Pebble® Plus

A Visit to The Library

Revised Edition

by Blake A. Hoena

CAPSTONE PRESS
a capstone imprint

Download the Capstone 4D app!

- Ask an adult to search in the Apple App Store or Google Play for "Capstone 4D".
- Click Install (Android) or Get, then Install (Apple).
- Open the app.
- Scan any of the following spreads with this icon:

When you scan a spread, you'll find fun extra stuff to go with this book!
You can also find these things on the web at www.capstone4D.com
using the password: **library.08307**

Pebble Plus is published by Capstone Press,
1710 Roe Crest Drive, North Mankato, Minnesota 56003
www.mycapstone.com

Copyright © 2018 by Capstone Press, a Capstone imprint.
All rights reserved. No part of this publication may be reproduced in whole or in part, or stored in a retrieval system, or transmitted in any form or by any means, electronic, mechanical, photocopying, recording, or otherwise, without written permission of the publisher

Library of Congress Cataloging-in-Publication Data
is available on the Library of Congress website.

ISBN 978-1-5435-0830-7 (library binding)
ISBN 978-1-5435-0842-0 (paperback)
ISBN 978-1-5435-0870-3 (ebook pdf)

Editorial Credits
Sarah Bennett, designer; Tracy Cummins, media researcher; Laura Manthe, production specialist

Photo Credits
Alamy: Randy Duchaine, 19; Capstone Press: Gary Sundermeyer, Cover, 3, 7, 11, 15, 21; Getty Images: Blend Images, 17; iStockphoto: asiseeit, 5, kali9, 13; Shutterstock: amirage, Design Element, Rob Marmion, 9

Note to Parents and Teachers

The A Visit to set supports national social studies standards related to the production, distribution, and consumption of goods and services. This book describes and illustrates a library. The images support early readers in understanding the text. The repetition of words and phrases helps early readers learn new words. This book also introduces early readers to subject-specific vocabulary words, which are defined in the Glossary section. Early readers may need assistance to read some words and to use the Table of Contents, Glossary, Read More, Internet Sites, Critical Thinking Questions, and Index sections of the book.

Printed in the United States 3958

Table of Contents

The Library 4

Using the Library 8

Librarians 12

Checking Out 16

Learning 20

- Glossary 22
- Read More 23
- Internet Sites 23
- Critical Thinking Questions 24
- Index 24

The Library

The library is a busy place to visit. Many people use the library every day.

The library is filled with shelves.

Each shelf holds many books.

Extreme Surfing
Purple
Mexico
espanol

Using the Library

Library visitors do research.

They use computers and books

to look for information.

Visitors sit quietly.

Some read books for fun.

Other visitors study.

The Last Mall Rat
POLICE CARS

Librarians

The library has many books to read. Librarians help visitors find the right book.

Librarians read picture books
during storytime.
Children and adults listen
to the story.

1
2
Summer
Jupiter
stars

Checking Out

Visitors can check out, or
borrow, books for a few weeks.
A library clerk scans
the visitor's library card.

FICTION
FREE SUMMER READING PROGRAM FOR ALL A

The library has many
other materials to check out.
Visitors borrow movies,
magazines, and audiobooks.

Lady and the Tramp
Lady and the Tramp
Friends Friends Together Again
Friends Friends Are Forever
Batman the Movie
Ninjago and Friends
Shrek
Shrek the Third
Shrek
The Smurfs
Sid's Pet Peeve
Sleeping Beauty
Marley & Me
Mary Poppins
Best of Percy
Thomas Gets
Tale of Brave
Puppets
Nanny and Christy
Keys of Friendship
Wild West
Night at Museum
Nanny McPhee
Zoo
Christmas

Learning

A library is a good place
to read and learn.

Sea
he Sea 1, 2, 3. Learn to count
a stars, octopuses, and
fun when you have colorful
rful foods, and other objects
nning readers can enjoy
acher or parent.
Titles in this series:
Baby Animals 1,2,3
A Counting Book of Animal Offspring
Eating Pairs
Counting Fruits and Vegetables by Twos
Under the Sea 1,2,3
Counting Ocean Life
3,2,1 Go!
A Transportation Countdown
Capstone
Under the Sea 1, 2, 3
Knox
Under the Sea
Counting Ocean Life
by Barbara Knox

Glossary

library card—a card with a person's name and library number printed on it; people use library cards to borrow materials from the library; they promise to bring back the materials on time and in good shape

materials—the items at a library that people can read or check out; magazines, newspapers, videos, CDs, audiobooks, and books are library materials

research—to look for; library visitors look for book titles or certain subjects on computers

scan—to use a machine that passes a beam of light over the code on a library card

storytime—a time when children and adults gather to listen to a story read out loud

Read More

Clark, Rosalyn. *A Visit to the Library.* Places We Go. Minneapolis: Lerner Publications, 2018.

Miller, Shannon McClintock. *Find a Book!* North Mankato, Minn.: Cantata Learning, 2018.

Siemens, Jared. *Librarian.* People in My Neighborhood. New York: Smartbook Media Inc., 2018.

Internet Sites

Use FactHound to find Internet sites related to this book.

Visit *www.facthound.com*

Just type **9781543508307** and go.

Critical Thinking Questions

1. What does a librarian do at the library?

2. Name some of the materials you can find at a library.

3. Describe what you like best about the library.

Index

adults, 14
borrow, 16, 18
check out, 16, 18
children, 14
computers, 8
information, 8
learn, 20
librarians, 12, 14
library card, 16
library clerk, 16
listen, 14
magazines, 18
materials, 18
movies, 18
quietly, 10
read, 10, 12, 14, 20
research, 8
scans, 16
shelf, 6
story, 14
study, 10